Buckingham and District

IN OLD PHOTOGRAPHS

Delivering the daily bread. Margaret and Vera Wootton look back from West Street in the 1930s. The old Bucks Hussars barracks are on the left.

Buckingham
and District

IN OLD PHOTOGRAPHS

ROBERT COOK

Budding BOOKS

A Budding Book

First published in 1994 by Alan Sutton
Publishing Limited

This edition published in 1998 by Budding Books,
an imprint of Sutton Publishing Limited
Phoenix Mill · Thrupp · Stroud · Gloucestershire
GL5 2BU

Copyright © Robert Cook, 1994

A catalogue record for this book is available from
the British Library

ISBN 1-84015-075-0

Typesetting and origination by
Sutton Publishing Limited.
Printed in Great Britain by
WBC Limited, Bridgend, Mid-Glamorgan.

Contents

Until five years ago a gilded swan stood on top of the eighteenth-century town hall. It became a county symbol, as can be seen on the side of this lorry which is involved in improvement works at the old cattle market in 1994. (© *Buckingham and Winslow Advertiser*)

Introduction

My old 'great grampy', Bill Cripps, used to say: 'You need one leg longer than the other to walk around Buckingham. It's a funny place, all ups and downs.' Like many old locals, Bill was plain speaking and some might take offence at that today. Certainly Buckingham, funny or not, has had a history full of ups and downs. But it had no name until Bucca's Saxon tribe landed by the river's bend. They came to farm, and called their new home Buccingahamme.

Chopping down woodland, they gained fuel for fires, building material for huts and created space for their fields. Had they known how to use the stone from so many Roman ruins scattered around the district they would have been better prepared for when the Danes invaded in 789. Instead they were clustered behind a wooden stockade on Castle Hill, where Alfred the Great made his headquarters for a while.

And so Buccingahamme gave its name to one of Alfred's new counties, organized to defend his kingdom. The district went on to prosper with the growing wool trade. When the Normans came, in 1066, they could not be bought off as their Danish forebears had often been. They imposed a new social order called feudalism, the influence of which lingers on. No place in England could escape it. Walter Giffard, the conqueror's son, became Earl of Buckingham and as a commissioner for the hated Domesday Book he was particularly unpopular.

Whatever the cruelties of the new regime, at least it was relieved by better architecture. Norman stonemasons created beauties including the chancel of Lillingstone Dayrell church and prelates as stately as Bishop de Craversende performed honours such as consecrating Winslow church in 1260.

England went from strength to strength from the Tudor age to the Renaissance. Buckingham remained a little too remote in the far north of the county to be affected by Henry VIII's plans for centralization. Thus the role of the county town passed south to Aylesbury, and Buckingham went its own way.

Always eccentric (some argue because the Celts were never entirely driven from the district when the Saxons came), Buckingham's population grew from 3,849 to 9,309 between 1864 and 1991. Many of the old buildings and old family names remain alongside new growth which followed the two world wars.

The shift of local government power from Buckingham Borough to Aylesbury Vale Council in 1974 created some suspicion and resentment. Certain subsequent 'improvements' to the centre have been criticized by a prominent town councillor as 'lacking in purpose and planning'. But Buckingham has never been famous for its planning. The Great Fire of 1725, which destroyed so much of the old, was followed by random growth creating

The days of the busy cattle market are long gone, but Aylesbury Council has done its bit to retain the charm. (© *Buckingham and Winslow Advertiser*)

narrow streets and some odd-shaped houses. In 1964 the Borough Council called for redevelopment, but little happened before 1974. Thereafter the town hall was sold and fell into decline, but Meadow Walk shopping precinct and a new car-park appeared in the town centre. The new shopkeepers were soon anxious about a Tesco superstore planned for the outskirts along London Road. Interested parties predicted death to the town centre.

These are early days to judge. The centre has been smartened up: the Old Gaol, famous for its castellations and stonework, is now a museum; visitors have a choice of car-parks and unusual shops. On the outskirts of Buckingham there is anxiety that the town is growing too fast towards surrounding villages, at great cost to the countryside.

In 1976 Margaret Thatcher (now Lady Thatcher) gave her support to, and opened, the country's first private university in Buckingham. In 1994, as its chancellor, she visited to collect an award for exporting her books and lectures. At that time she commented: 'Buckingham is a charming town.' In spite of everything that has happened to it over the years, there are many who would agree with her.

Robert Cook, September 1994

SECTION ONE
An Old Market Town

A quiet town centre in the late 1940s. Looking north from the town hall, W.H. Smith is on the left; it is still on this site.

Car parts manufacturer Wipac replaced its 1960s' edifice with modern offices, alongside a new Tesco superstore, in the early 1990s. (© *Buckingham and Winslow Advertiser*)

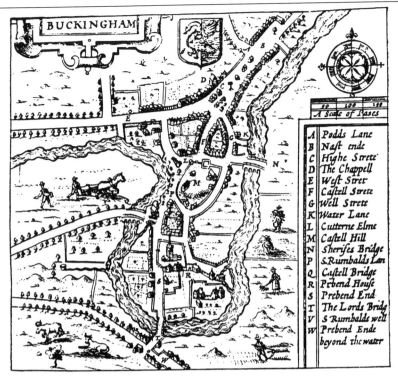

John Speed's map of Buckingham, 1610.

Buckingham market place in the late nineteenth century. The Aylesbury Brewery is on the right and Lord Cobham's gift of a gaol looks menacing in the background (centre, right).

Buckingham Bullring, 1910.

Iron Bridge in Ford Street, early 1900s. The football field is behind the fence and the eighteenth-century church of St Peter and Paul is visible in the distance.

Well Street, early 1930s. The school is in the centre, with Kiddy Halton's antique shop on the left and the Bull pub on the right. Flooding was frequent and provided some fun for drummer Jackie Larnder's dog when it wasn't chasing schoolchildren.

A Sunday morning in Castle Street, late nineteenth century. Note the thatched cottages on the right; these are no longer there.

Grandmother Bertha Tunks from Lenborough Road, early 1930s. Des Tunks (to her right) recalls that 'Sunday wasn't Sunday if you didn't go and visit Gran.'

The old post office (centre) dominates this view of West Street from the early 1900s.

Postman Albert Osborne used to cycle out to Dadford and deliver mail to the Comte de Paris while he was living at Stowe. The Comte leased Stowe after the Duke of Buckingham went abroad in 1848. The Comte was Louis Philippe's grandson and pretender to the French throne. He died at Stowe in 1894. Dadford used to be within the Stowe grounds until the duke had it moved.

In 1945 Buckingham RDC Councillor T.R. Osborne strongly protested against the appointment of a rodent officer at £250 per annum plus travelling expenses. He decided that if such a scheme were carried out he would 'never enter that room again'. The most effective way of destroying rats was to offer a price for tails and to prosecute people who had rat-infested property and did nothing about it. No doubt Buckingham Ratting Club, pictured here in the 1920s, would have agreed.

Buckingham Paint Factory (the Old Castle Mill) after the fire of November 1964. Disgruntled labourer Raymond Weighell flooded the factory with white spirit and set it alight. The first explosion was heard just before midnight and firemen were called from throughout the county. Weighell owned up and the insurance company paid for a new purpose-built factory.

Brackley Road Cemetery, 1938. Preparations are being made for the funeral of Mr 'Doughie' Plank, owner of the Nelson Street Bakery.

In 1953 a gentleman popped into the White Hart and forthrightly told the management that its statue's antlers were on back to front and were the wrong sort, and that he would send some more. They arrived the next day with a note from the Duke of Bedford. Unfortunately they were stolen in 1984.

Christmas goodies on sale in Nelson Street, 1891. The small boy on the far right is Tom Tailby, son of a Castle Street greengrocer.

A view of the town hall (centre, left) from Bridge Street, 1897. The gilded swan is just visible on the top of the building.

Let's hope W.H. Thomas was master as well as jack of all trades. Diversification was certainly his strong point.

Markham's was the biggest and best general hardware and ironmonger's in the district, and was crucial to a farming community. It was a mainstay of the town until its closure and conversion to a wine shop in the 1980s.

Marshall Herring's sold all you needed for a smart horse! It is pictured in around 1904.

Arthur 'I say' Marriott, a popular local figure, sold and repaired all sorts of pedal and motor bikes in his Castle Street shop. He traded for sixty years, working into his eighties, and is seen here in 1986.

The firm of Arthur's late brother Amos continues to trade in the old Bullring (now the Market Place). This picture shows it in its early days, c. 1922.

William Horace Wootton at his Nelson Street bakery, 1920s. Though self-taught, his cake-making was outstanding. His son Albert did not wish to continue the business and it was sold in 1950.

Master cake-maker William Wootton at work.

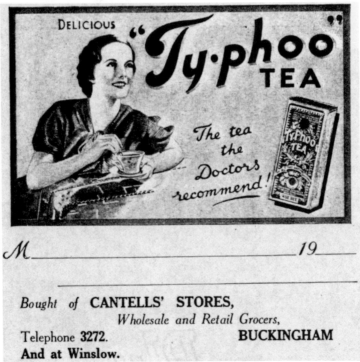

Those were the days! Interestingly tea is once again being commended as a healthy product. The receipt dates from the 1930s, but the Winslow shop still trades under the old family name.

Very quaint but out of date: in 1964 Buckingham Borough Council advised shop owners of a need to redevelop the town centre because it was 'out of date'. This site is now the entrance to Meadow Walk shopping precinct.

Twist!

Sarongster lets you!

VYLE'S of BUCKINGHAM
have them !

Only Sarongster moves with you, not against you—thanks to patented Criss-Cross Control. Lets you Twist. Bend. Even stretch. Because Sarongster's overlapping front panels give you complete freedom. No restriction at the thigh. No binding seams down the middle. So now you can Twist to your heart's content . . . in Sarongster. Come in and try them!

Illustrated:
Sarongster
Dip Front   **28/6**

Also: Cuff Waist 37/6;   High Waist 42/-;   Pantie Brief 39/6.

A modern image in the advert but Vyle's shop was also 'out of date' and closed in June 1962.

The first of the new shops in Market Square. Record crowds gathered for the opening of Woolworth's in March 1964, but Mrs H. Hutt and D. Flower were the first customers.

In 1964 Scotland Yard was called in to investigate the death of a woman found by the railway viaduct on a quiet stretch of the River Ouse. The local constabulary was based at Moreton Road. Incidents involving a bolting horse and a tramp had prompted the County Council to build the police station there in 1892. The old gaol ceased to be a lock-up and the borough police merged with the county constabulary. This was just as well, with crime increasing.

Thew, Hooker and Gilby knew how to fatten a Saddleback pig at their Chandos Road piggery, which adjoined the milk factory. The photograph dates from 1934.

Tom Mallet used to drive his lorry around local farms in the 1920s before leaving to drive long distance for a local brickyard. His former employers, Thew, Hooker and Gilby, were subsequently taken over by Wilts United Dairies. Tom was elected mayor and magistrate after the war.

United Dairies driver George Cracknell worked long hours, taking his loads as far as London. The firm even delivered cream to Buckingham Palace. In his spare time George kept up a family tradition of excellence at football, and he was in both the works and town teams. He is seen here in 1931.

United Dairies driver Bill Tomkins started as a trailer boy operating a special brake while the driver struggled with the main controls. But liquid loads were difficult to transport in the 1920s as this London Road incident demonstrates. Sergeant Small arrived by bicycle to take charge.

Buckets of water couldn't stop Buckingham's Great Fire of 1725 destroying most of Castle Street. The wind fanned flames on to Market Hill. A third of the town's 387 houses were destroyed, prompting investment in a proper fire brigade. Here is the force of 1884 based at the Engine House. The site is now occupied by Barclay's Bank.

The County Council took over the fire service in 1948 and soon Buckingham had this modern engine and new premises at North End, on the workhouse site.

The Imperial Yeomanry on Market Hill before leaving for the South African War, 1899.

Not a Charlie Chaplin look-alike competition but 'Dad's Army' 1914 style, parading on Market Hill. Note the shops boarded up for protection against bomb blasts, should German Zeppelins reach this far.

Brickworkers from the Calvert yard at a dinner laid on by the London Brick Co., in Buckingham Town Hall, *c*. 1947.

The Royal Naval Band 'beating the retreat' towards Buckingham Town Hall, October 1950.

Buckingham station was still very busy in the 1950s. Milk from the neighbouring dairy made up a large proportion of the goods transported, as can be seen from this picture.

Buckingham has had a few town halls in its time. One was a lean-to in the Castle grounds. Here is a full frontal view of the biggest and best, still going strong after quite a lot of social use in the 1940s. A gift from the Temple family of Stowe, it is currently undergoing refurbishment after several changes of owner.

Village and Countryside

Margaret Walker was the forester's daughter living on Verney's Claydon Estate early this century. She remembers having the freedom to roam the lanes and fields, following the hunt and walking over a mile to school in Botolph Claydon. 'There were few cars, we had respect for adults and no fear of being molested. Sir Harry Verney had a big Morris and sometimes drove us into Winslow. When he went over bridges we'd bounce off our seats and he'd chortle "ha ha". We were well fed, never cheeked our mother or went short of what we needed.' But as this picture shows, big changes were on the way. Over a thousand horses a week were loaded at Winslow station, en route for a 'war to end all wars'. The countryside and villages would never be the same again.

Old Cottage. Adstock. Bucks.

Labouring families once shivered and crowded into these Adstock cottages before the days of improvement grants and trendy conversions. Clergy chosen by ruling aristocrats comforted the poor. One wonders what form this took from Adstock rector Thomas Egerton, whose wife Sarah wrote in 1686: 'Shall I be one of those obsequious fools/ That square by custom's scanty rules?'

Customs change. This church at Akeley was demolished in the early 1980s because locals were not interested in fund raising to save its crumbling tower.

The Planks near Addington, viewed from a then-busy Oxford–Cambridge railway line, 1907. Clay in this area exacerbates flooding.

Discipline was clear and simple in the old days and few stepped out of line. Here are Addington stocks, 1908.

A morale-boosting service at Calvert brickworks football stadium, 1940. One man seems to be getting his spirit from a bottle.

It looks as if this child is wearing her Sunday best in this pretty scene from East Claydon, 1908.

East Claydon again. Doesn't this boy look a little angel? 'But we weren't,' said local Margaret Rogers. 'We went scrumping.' Sad to leave her village school, Margaret hated the Royal Latin School in Buckingham, where a teacher called her a 'lovesick swain' for walking out with a boyfriend. 'And *he'd* had an affair with a pupil.'

This seat, built around a tree, was given to East Claydon by Mr F.M. Verney in 1912. Believed to be the only one of its kind in Britain, the left-hand picture shows the tree as little more than a sapling, growing through the roof in 1931. The right-hand picture shows it in a poor state in the 1950s.

This poster from the late nineteenth century evokes memories of an age when firemen had to be knocked up, sometimes mistook sunsets for conflagration and still had to run and catch the horses before they could go anywhere.

MIDDLE CLAYDON
Parish Council Fire Brigade.

Authorized Charges.

The Brigade and use of Engine to be paid for as follows :—Use of Engine £5 5s. with horses, for outside Middle Claydon, and £3 10s. 0d. with horses, in Middle Claydon ; Brigade, 12s. 0d. per hour ; for three hours or under, £2 ; Pumpers, first hour 1s. 6d., each following hour 1/- ; Refreshments at discretion of Superintendent.

The charges for the Engine and Brigade to be submitted by the Superintendent to the Fire Brigade Committee, before payment be demanded.

J. BRENNAN, Superintendent.
A. COX, 2nd Officer.
W. H. BLINDELL, Clerk.

A. J. CLEAR, PRINTER, WINSLOW.

A frosty morning at the bridge over Granborough Brook early this century.

Peace and tranquillity outside the Crown Inn, Granborough, before the First World War.

The approach to Great Horwood and not a car in sight. How it has changed in ninety years: the market-place now makes a fine car-park. Claims to fame include William Warham, who was rector in 1487 and went on to become Archbishop of Canterbury, crowning Henry VIII.

The buying and selling, the old fortune telling. A tinker's cart passes through Great Horwood in the late nineteenth century.

Once upon a time most people dressed for Sunday, like this handsome fellow posing by Great Horwood Brook. Today's commuter rush has meant a wider bridge and no time for onlookers in the middle of the road.

Little Horwood has grown, but not too large, in recent years. Building plots are at a premium. There is a great sense of community as this village fête in the early 1970s suggests.

The A413 connects London, Aylesbury, Buckingham and main villages. Here it is blocked by snow between Lillingstone Lovell and the northern county border in the 1930s. Note the well-kept road sign.

This interesting bridge was on the Grand Union Canal at Maids Moreton. Built two hundred years ago, the canal is now no more than a grassy dip in the landscape. Running through Foscote, Thornton, Deanshanger and Old Stratford, it once carried coal, gravel and other raw materials into, and farm produce and industrial goods out of, Buckingham. Usurped by railways, the wharf house is now a builder's merchant's.

Sir Gilbert Scott declared Maids Morton church tower to be 'of admirable and unique design'. It suffered at Cromwell's hands but perhaps no more so than this road has from modern traffic. Maids Moreton post office is in the foreground.

Elizabeth Owen's father, a thatcher, walked miles from the pretty village of Padbury for work. 'Him and gramp were on Verney's estate. When they said they wouldn't vote for him [c. 1902], Verney said, "Pack up and don't come again." '

Old End, Padbury, in the late nineteenth century. Thank God for Anglian Water. Even if springs were purer, it was hard work on that old pump.

Padbury Mill was once a busy place but the miller's tale was of hard work and little profit. Charles Crook ceased milling here in 1931.

Bertha Allan, in charge of Padbury station, sees three of her children off to Buckingham School in the 1950s.

The sun is shining on Padbury and the train will soon arrive: a scene from the 1950s. For many the bus service was more convenient so the station's days were numbered. It closed to passengers in 1967.

Henry and Esmie (née Wootton) Thomas (standing, left) with proud grandparents after christening their first child at Preston Bissett in the 1950s. Church traditions mattered then.

Preston Bissett teenager Doris Bull pictured just before the Second World War.

Happily married to Harry (standing behind), Doris Bull relaxes for a family snapshot in 1972. Some say Preston Bissett's roads have never been as clean since Harry retired from his roadman's job.

Shalstone village is 4 miles west of Buckingham and is very quiet in this 1950s' scene.

John Turvey, farm labourer from Swanbourne, and his family. His efforts to form a union caused him problems with the gentry late last century.

Thornborough village was a farming community long before the Normans came. This is 1904 and another world. Men took Sunday dinners to the bakehouse, then in Sunday best waited in two groups under different trees, chatting until it was time for church or chapel. After the service they collected their dinners, ready cooked.

Thornborough stocks met a sorry end in the 1930s when Thomas Dillow, living in a hut by the pond, chopped them up for firewood.

This view of Thornborough Mill in the 1970s shows it well on the way to becoming a luxury home and is a far cry from the days of toil, when the Great Ouse drove the waterwheel. Milling ceased here in 1962.

Grindstones inside Thornborough Mill.

Frank Taylor, the miller, found this poster on a barn wall at the mill. It is advertising horse-racing at Thornborough, an event now defunct.

A miller could not live by bread alone. Caravaning boomed in the 1950s and the Taylors established a camp-site. This visitor is enjoying the view south from Thornborough Mill.

Young folk enjoy Thornborough's country views and air in the 1960s.

Tingewick telegraph boys pose for the camera, 1903.

Tingewick in the late 1940s, before the juggernauts took over. Though approved, a bypass has not been built because residents have protested that the proposed route would run too close to their homes.

Simons' Stores, Tingewick. Before the war this village shop sold everything a country person needed. But modern country folk need so much they have to drive to town and village stores decline.

The Power and the Glory

Claydon House, rebuilt after the Civil War, is viewed here from the south, *c.* 1917. This was the seat of the Verney family who, together with the Church, had a formative influence on the district. After the Second World War, however, new fortunes and socialist challenges persuaded Major Ralph Verney to abandon liberalism and join a socialist crusade. Not that national politics ever really worried most Buckingham folk; perhaps they only used their freedom for the sake of novelty when they chose 'man of the people' Robert Maxwell for MP. Safe again in Tory hands since 1970, the only political matter seriously to trouble the town was the 1974 Local Government Reform, when the *Advertiser* reported: 'It is sad but true, we have to face the fact that we must now begin to look to Aylesbury for our main local government attention.'

Sir Harry Verney and family at Claydon House, early 1900s. This was a family that cared for the district; Sir Harry's son Sir Ralph (standing to his left) successfully saved Claydon School from closure in 1989.

J.G. Hubbard, later Lord Addington, gave the town a hospital in 1886. Saved from closure in 1977, it is now well equipped for emergencies. Curiously, the establishment once received a pair of Queen Victoria's bloomers as a gift.

Secret Ballot and Universal Manhood Suffrage Acts made this election of 1897 a change from the bribery and corruption of Buckingham's 'rotten borough' days. The winner was Carlile, the Conservative candidate, who gained 5,266 votes – a majority of 430. Reading results from the White Hart balcony became a tradition.

Tom Smith's pub, the Three Cups, was convenient for the town hall opposite. For fifty-three years he was first to vote and would open up at 5 a.m. to serve refreshments to chauffeurs collecting passengers from the hunt ball. He died in 1950.

Lord Addington lived at Addington Manor. This building was replaced by something less fantastic in 1933. But echoes of Addington's words linger. In 1870, he said: 'People who never took any part in education themselves, all at once are seized with an irresistible idea of spreading over the whole country what they call a National System of education. A more cruel and obvious injustice to the poor was never perpetrated.'

A serene Seven Gables on the edge of Addington estate, 1910.

Stowe, now a public school, was designed by Vanbrugh and Kent for Sir Richard Temple in the seventeenth century. The house is over 900 ft long, with two wings. Stowe Avenue, leading from Buckingham to the Corinthian arch, was one of the finest avenues of beeches and elms in the country.

The lodge gates in the nineteenth century. Woe betide anyone caught poaching in the grounds. Lord Cobham is said to have sent two men back dead.

Through the years Stowe was the home or haven for the rich or royal. This scene shows a gay pair approaching the arches in a newfangled motor car in the 1920s.

William Lowndes bought Winslow Manor between 1697 and 1709. His great hall was built in 1700 with locally made bricks. This view is looking across Home Close and Sheep Street, early 1900s. Norman McCorquodale bought the estate in 1897 and sold it for housing development in the 1950s.

McCorquodale's limousine was supplied and maintained by Phillips & Sons, of Chandos Road. The car is pictured in front of the garages at Winslow Hall.

Chetwode Manor gardens, 1912. The manor was once owned by the Chetwode family, who are said to have been granted the right of an annual fair after they slayed a terrible wild boar in Chetwode woods. A mound dug up in 1810 revealed the skeleton of a huge boar.

Chetwode church and priory was converted from the chancel of an Augustinian priory, built in 1240. It is a fine example of early English workmanship, with a graceful five-lancet east window covering nearly the whole wall.

Many regard Hillesden church as Buckingham's finest. It was built in the fifteenth century by the monks of Notley Abbey. The Denton family bought Hillesden manor in 1547. Sir Alexander came to grief following an attack in 1643 by Cromwell's Roundheads, and was imprisoned and died in the Tower of London. Musket-ball marks are still visible on the north porch door, though little remains of the original stained glass.

Rehanging the bells at Winslow church, 1929. They were made in Buckingham during the seventeenth century.

Charles Langley, head groom at Captain Lambton's Redfield Estate at the turn of the century.

Captain Lambton bought Redfield and 170 acres for £17,500 in 1885. Polo was regularly played in the grounds and Lambton kept a large stable of ponies and hunters. The house and estate were sold to the county council for £15,500 in 1946.

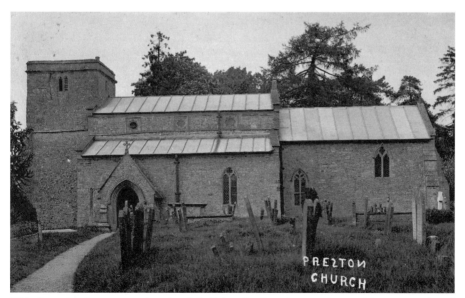

This fourteenth-century church of St John the Baptist stands on rising ground and commands a fine view of the countryside surrounding Preston Bissett.

A record crowd gathered for the election of March 1950. Mayor Markham had warned of socialist 'lies' but still Labour's Aidan Crawley managed a second victory, with a 1,654 majority. The *Daily Mail* reported: 'Labour is back in office but not in power. This Government is on a razor's edge.'

Labour leader Hugh Gaitskell visiting a Buckingham fund-raising event, June 1962.

Following the hunt through Granborough in the late nineteenth century.

Otter-hunting in front of Thornborough Mill, late 1930s. Frank Taylor recalled: 'I never saw a live otter in my life but I saw a dead one thrown up in the air for the hounds to eat.'

Councillor Cornwall became Mayor of Buckingham in May 1962, aged twenty-eight. He was the youngest mayor in the town's history.

Mr and Mrs Robert Maxwell during his election campaign in 1964. His slogan, 'Let Harold and Bob finish the job', captured the imagination of Buckingham folk and his success amazed the defeated Conservatives.

SECTION FOUR

Wheels and Wings

Horses and carts could just about squeeze through Winslow High Street in 1908. Although built by Wren, the old market house (left) was demolished to make room for the larger buses and cars of the 1950s. In the 1930s motor vehicles multiplied faster than rabbits and plans were made to accommodate them. The impact on Buckinghamshire communities was enormous and soon tranquillity was gone. Even overhead, engines throbbed. First World War fighters landed near Padbury and early aviators crashed in fields. The airship R101 was tested around the area (see p. 71), then the Second World War came and disaster struck Winslow when an RAF training flight crashed on Winslow High Street (see p. 73). Following the declaration of peace an old wartime aerodrome at Silverstone became a race track (see p. 75) and cars flooded along the A413, clogging up Buckingham, to watch the sport.

Addington Park, early 1900s. It is still a very quiet place.

Delivering ale to Granborough's pubs was a job for stout horses and strong men in the late nineteenth century.

Phillips & Sons began coachbuilding in Preston Bissett, moving from the Pound (now Willow Garage) to Buckingham early this century. Here is a fine example of their work, made to a design supplied by the Bucks Hussars and bound for the First World War.

The company soon adapted to the motor age, supplying and servicing the cars of those wealthy enough to afford them.

This plane has just landed near Windmill Hill, Charndon, 1912. It is believed to be the first one to have landed in the district.

Doomed airship R101, meant to be an imperial flagship, passed over Horn Street, Winslow, on a test flight from Cardington, 1930. Lou Pottier remembers the teacher taking children out of class to watch it pass low and noisily overhead: 'You felt as if you could touch it.' The R101 crashed at Beauvais, France, in October 1930.

A child was killed as she ran in front of Reg Baldwin's Buckingham-bound bus in the summer of 1933. The Granborough house was badly damaged but fortunately a baby inside was saved.

Frank Taylor bought this Ford lorry in the 1930s. Apart from delivering corn meal, he developed a coal business which traded until 1946.

Tragedy struck Winslow High Street at 3 a.m. on 7 August 1943. A Wellington bomber from the 92nd Operational Training Unit, Great Horwood, clipped a walnut tree and crashed into houses, killing seventeen people. George Hawkins was one of the brigade called to the fierce fire. His father, a blacksmith, was among the dead.

War planes were lost at an alarming rate and fund raising was continuous. As a finale to all the struggle and sacrifice Winslow held a Wings Week. The *Buckingham Advertiser* reported: 'It was a mammoth procession to the market square; one of the largest in the history of the town and led by an RAF band.'

RAF aircrews were all volunteers and wore their wings with pride. Wartime marriages often combined great romance and tragedy. Married at Winslow in 1943, Peggy Gordon Dean lost both her navigator husband and pilot brother in the conflict.

This new Fordson Major was available from a Buckingham dealer during the war years. It eased the toil of the back-breaking farmwork undertaken by an army of land-girls, many of whom were new to the countryside.

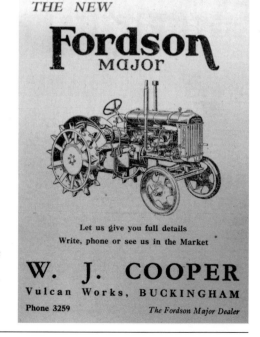

Wartime pilots earned their wings at Silverstone. The old abbey once stood within the airfield boundaries in an age when only angels flew. After the war the airfield went from wings to wheels but daring deeds continued, as demonstrated by this shot of racers leaving Abbey Curve during the first Grand Prix, 1948.

Stirling Moss makes a pit stop at the British Grand Prix, 1954. Is that Murray Walker in the background?

Hazel Rawlings, all set for a trip from Calvert to Buckingham, late 1950s.

You see more Austins on the roads of Britain today than any other single make of car

The A40 — a champion dollar earner for Britain

Many of the old Austins still very actively employed have withstood rough treatment as well as years of hard work. A Brecknockshire owner tells of his 1933 Austin 'Ten'—

"*In 1940 her remains lay beneath the debris of a garage. An optimist salvage man tried to start her—and she worked. During the war she received shocking treatment in all weathers and on every type of road without missing a beat.*"

The new Austin A40 'Devon' has the same hardy constitution; it, too, will prove that . . .

This is a 1933 Austin 'Ten' of the type mentioned

AN **AUSTIN** LASTS LONGER
— you can depend on it !

Agents—

PHILLIPS & SONS (Buckingham) Ltd

Motor Works, Buckingham

Phone—Buckingham 2121   Telegrams—Phillips Buckingham

You could, and still can, buy the latest models from Phillips & Sons. This advertisement dates from 1952.

Car enthusiast Michael Sellar posing in front of an MGA on Winslow Market Square, 1950s. It is Silverstone race day and racegoers regularly stopped for refreshments at the old Bell Inn (in the background, left) before rejoining the throng on the A413.

Young Michael never had a pedal car as good as this – but who did? Still, he loved cars and went on to work in Phillips & Sons' body shop.

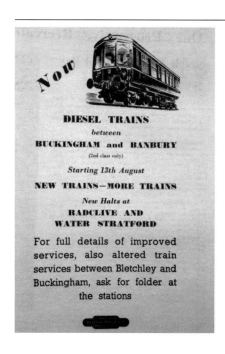

Now

DIESEL TRAINS
between
BUCKINGHAM and BANBURY
(2nd class only)

Starting 13th August

NEW TRAINS—MORE TRAINS

New Halts at
**RADCLIVE AND
WATER STRATFORD**

For full details of improved services, also altered train services between Bletchley and Buckingham, ask for folder at the stations

Diesel railcars were introduced by British Railways as an experiment to cut costs in the 1950s. Like buses, they needed fewer staff, less fuel and were flexible. Nevertheless, the experiment was cut short, the lines closed and the future given over to motor vehicles.

The Red Rover Bus Company was still earning a good living when this picture was taken outside Lord Cobham's famous gaol. On market days it collected so many passengers through the villages that a relief bus would follow to collect the overflow.

Many coach companies started up between the wars and day-tripping was in its heyday. Payne's prospered, although this picture shows a minor setback when their High Street garage caught fire in February 1959. Fred Douglas heard the first explosion from his neighbouring cottage, where he was watching the television. The glow could be seen for miles around but only one coach was scorched.

Haulage contractors boomed, too. This lorry at Phillips & Sons' motor works was always busy around the local lanes. It is pictured in 1970.

Girl on a motor cycle. Ena Rackliff tries out her father's BSA at Calvert, 1950s.

SECTION FIVE

Hard Labour

At the start of this century farming was still the main industry, and here, foresters are working on the Claydon Estate. Another prominent industry in the area was brickmaking, which was revolutionized when Arthur Itter opened his deep claypits at Calvert; these were sited near the railway for ease of transport. Railways, too, offered a range of opportunities. Employment was also provided by the thriving quarries around Thornton; these supplied stone to church and house builders. There is a myth that because folk worked so hard for little pay, they could not be happy. But people found pleasures and usually accepted their place. Many acquired great skills and took satisfaction from doing a good job. The biggest changes to employment were brought about by the motor vehicle, which created some jobs and destroyed others.

Even the vicar has popped into the picture. On the estate wood was cut, measured and sawn for posts and rails; much of it was sent to sawmills.

John Walker joined the Claydon Estate in 1914 and was over seventy when he retired fifty years later. His daughter Margaret remembers him as a lovely man who always worked hard for his family.

Mark Brain, Claydon Estate gardener, 1920s. He always gave a friendly greeting and was a genius with flowers – making both garden and home bright and cheerful.

Building a swimming-pool by the East Claydon–Winslow road, early 1900s. The site was near the present power station. The pool was demolished in the 1930s.

East Claydon at the turn of the century. Roadmen are filling in potholes before the age of tarmac. Curiously, when electricity came to the village in the 1930s, the one gas street light was removed and not replaced.

Itter's claypit, 1903. Men worked on terraces, levering out great lumps of clay with iron bars. The landslide (centre, left) shows the obvious dangers.

Threshing at Scott's Lane, Maids Moreton, 1910.

Clay has been moved from the pit to brick-pressing shops by various means over the years. Here is driver Harry Webb and his 'Black Gang', which operated the yard shunting engine in 1927. The name of the engine, *Phorpres*, referred to the way bricks were pressed four times.

Building the railway cutting at Charndon, 1897.

Bryant Bros of Preston Bissett displaying their modern fleet in the 1930s. In the 1960s their red tippers were eye catching, but never more so than when the cab of one was placed by a hedge on the Tingewick road. The firm had donated it to a roadman for shelter.

Pip Askham (left) and shunter Walter Newman taking a breather in the early 1930s at what might have been a busier Verney Junction had Sir Harry's Channel Tunnel dream come true. Sir Harry promoted his railway link when a channel tunnel was mooted in the late 1840s. He and his fellow railway directors imagined that people would change trains and stop over at Verney Junction. Consequently he built the Verney Arms.

Farmer Gerald Thomas does the rounds at his Preston Bissett farm on a Beardmore motor bike, 1920.

Gerald Thomas ready for night duty with the Royal Observer Corps. He would probably have seen German bombers swarming across North Bucks for their raid on Coventry.

Charlie Whitehall and Norman Capel looking fit and ready for honest toil at Thornborough Mill, 1930s.

One of their regular jobs was weed cutting along the river so as to keep a good flow on the water-wheel. Sawing across the river with a long chain fastened to scythes, first they cut below the mill; otherwise too much water would collect and cause flooding.

Threshing at Thornborough Mill, after the Second World War. Voluntary labour from all over the country was still vital to farming at that time.

Frank Taylor farmed about 40 acres at Thornborough, and sheep shearing was part of his routine. He is pictured before the war.

Was there no ending to Frank Taylor's talents? I don't think pig racing ever caught on in Thornborough!

With dog Candy on board, farmer's son Bob Dickins is all set for a day's ploughing at Hanover Farm on the Addington Estate, early 1950s.

Traditional Buckinghamshire lacemaking at Redfield, near Winslow, 1899.

Porter Ben Cadd admires the gold wristwatch awarded to Buckingham Station Master Whitney, to mark forty-five years of railway service, December 1959. Ben once observed: 'I spent thirty years as a navy petty officer. Little did I know I was coming here to be a lady's lavatory attendant.'

Brick lorries from the Calvert yard were a colourful sight along highways and byways from the 1930s till 1991. Pictured in the 1970s, Howard Payne (left) was the last man in charge of their maintenance.

SECTION SIX

Play Days

Addington Lake has not frozen over for a long time. Perhaps global warming is the reason. However, there were few pleasures to beat skating when these pictures were taken in the winter of 1907. As a child Gladys Close remembered it as a highlight of Christmas, recalling that 'Doctor Leapingwell and his daughter were lovely skaters.' And in the summer girls played cricket alongside the boys, though football remained a male preserve. Other forms of entertainment were country sports and amateur theatricals. Variety was provided by the arrival of strolling players, circuses and funfairs. In the 1920s films brought images from other places and motor coaches allowed people to seek more distant pleasures. And through all the changes some traditions remain, like Pancake Day races and Buckingham Fair.

Buckingham Pig Roast, 1906. A fat bullock was also roasted by a professional ox roaster and a fireman was on hand. Proceeds of £28 10s went to Buckingham Nursing Home.

Outside Buckingham Conservative Club, celebrating George V and Queen Mary's visit, 1927. All the decorations had to be made twice because they blew down in gales the night before. This was the last royal visit to Buckingham until the Queen Mother opened the new Royal Latin School on her way to Stowe in 1963.

Singleborough cricket team during peace celebrations, 1919.

Thew, Hooker and Gilby's milk factory football team at home, 1920s.

Steeple Claydon football team at home, 1952.

Jim Murden, claypit foreman at Calvert brickworks, 1950s. Jim was a country and nature lover and the claypit made an excellent habitat for him to explore.

Miss Thurlow and other members of a local thespian group re-enact a hold-up along the Banbury Road, 1957.

Canon Beamish leads an outing of choirboys from St Laurence's church, Winslow, to the countryside, 1950s.

AIR TRAINING CORPS (1563 Squadron)

Dance

Town Hall, Buckingham

Saturday, January 6th, 1945

BLUE EAGLES DANCE BAND

Admission 3/-, Forces 2/-   8—11.30 p.m.

Lighting Effects   *Right of admission reserved*

Buckingham Town Hall was a haven for dance and romance during the war years. With so much new blood in the district there was bound to be excitement.

Henry Smith was a popular pianist throughout the wartime years. Here he celebrates what would have been one of the first social events at the new British Legion Hall, Winslow, in the 1950s. He often played at Buckingham Town Hall events.

The Buckingham Electric Cinema was showing *The Coveted Heritage* at the town hall in March 1916. Seat prices started at 3*d*. However, there was no permanent cinema until Walter Parker opened the Chandos, in January 1934. The first film shown, *This Week of Grace*, starred Gracie Fields.

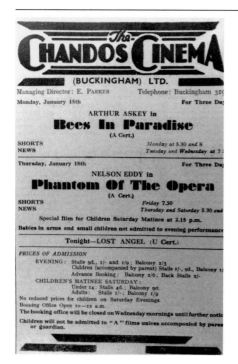

Mr Parker built on early success in the Midlands but did not live to see the post-war queues along Chandos Road. He died in 1940 and his daughter Gwen became the mainstay of a facility which provided so much pleasure to many, until the changes brought about by the construction of Milton Keynes and the age of the video. The cinema became a car lot in the 1980s.

Here we see the trials and tribulations of a learner Bentley driver being filmed at Buckingham Golf Club, for a comedy called *The Fast Lady*, 1950s.

Reg Goodwin (standing, far right), manager of Calvert brickworks, and colleagues taking one of their regular fishing trips to the Claydon lakes on a summer Sunday, early 1950s.

The Order of Water Buffalos provides a children's Christmas party at Winslow Public Hall, 1950s.

Wilfred Pickles and his radio team from *Have a Go* at Buckingham Town Hall, January 1964.

Women line up for the traditional Pancake Day race, February 1964.

The Caribbean sound of a traditional steel band charmed villagers at Twyford Fête, 1973. Here some of the band members are enjoying the fête's other attractions.

Buckingham Fair is based on a 440-year-old charter, which has survived years of plague and famine. This photograph from the 1980s shows the pleasure it still provides.

SECTION SEVEN

Happiest Days

Esmie and William 'Grampy' Wootton haymaking by the tennis court. It must have been fun in all that sunshine. Like most traders, Grampy kept a horse to pull a delivery cart – and a working horse needed lots of hay. Those were happy days, indeed; Esmie was born at the baker's shop and watched her grandfather perform miracles with his cakes. Life at Miss Denchfield's private school in Chandos Road was good, but moving on to the big school in London Road was rather frightening. In the end most Buckingham children turned out all right. Teachers were strict but they were usually caring and were respected.

Youngsters cluster around Buckingham's North End water pump, 1908. They wouldn't dream of vandalizing it!

It must have pleased these children that snowploughs had not been invented. They are enjoying the fruits of a heavy fall on Horn Street, Winslow, 1907.

The gymnastics class from the Buckingham Evening School after their display, 1909. W.J. Dolman (far right) and W. Dunkley were the instructors.

Shipton Brook was a fine fishing ground for tiddlers. It was also a good place for watching the weary cart-horses drink. This photograph dates from around 1908.

Dolly and George Berry outside their parents' pub, the Nag's Head, in Sheep Street, Winslow, c. 1932. Market days filled the tiny tap room to bursting, old boys aired their dialect, sucked their clay pipes, drank plenty and bashed away at skittles.

Steeple Claydon village school, 1906. Here children were taught to be God-fearing and to respect their elders.

Dadford village school near Stowe, early 1900s.

Buckingham Infant School, 1920s.

Winslow National School, 1914. Pupils are helping to 'dig for victory'. Food supplies were seriously threatened by German U-Boats and cultivating school gardens gave these boys a wartime role.

Sergeant Small's children outside Steeple Claydon police house, 1922. Bill (second from left) went on to train as a barber in Buckingham before opening his own shop in Winslow in the late 1940s.

The Read children on holiday at lacemakers' cottages in Buckingham just after the First World War. Bill made a career in broadcasting and also earned a wide reputation for his excellent pottery in Winslow.

Ena Rackliff explores the leafy lanes around 1940s' Calvert in an age when it was still fairly safe to do so.

There is now a dental surgery at these premises in Winslow High Street, I hope not repairing too many damaged teeth caused by sweet-eating such as this.

Glad Close and cousin Stan Blake walking down Little Horwood Road towards Winslow School, 1928.

Stan Blake tries the farmer's rake for size, and over the fence are Winslow School's not so convenient conveniences. The boys' section had no roof so it was unsafe to stand too close to the outside wall without an umbrella!

Temporary HORSAs (Hutting Operation for Raising the School Leaving Age) stand new behind these excellent specimens of the nation's future, early 1950s. Two of these huts were in use up to the school's closure in 1991.

Buckingham children on a trip organized by the Transport and General Workers Union, 1950. They were off to see a pantomime.

Thornton College tennis players, 1950s. This establishment has always upheld the highest traditions of education for young ladies.

Winslow School pupils giving a fine performance for parents at the old public hall in 1952.

Competitors in Gawcott Horticultural Show fancy-dress parade after judging, August 1952.

This twelfth-century chantry chapel survived the Great Fire and is the oldest building in Buckingham. It was home to the Royal Latin School until it moved to Chandos Road in 1907.

Mrs Creighton, art teacher of the Royal Latin School in the early 1950s. In the words of an ex-pupil, Grace Durham: 'She was a lovely person and a brilliant teacher.'

Royal Latin School girls, exams behind them and a world awaiting, 1956. Grace Durham (front, centre) now runs her own coach company.

Mr Evans, remembered as a much-loved music teacher, was the driving-force behind Gilbert and Sullivan productions at the Royal Latin School during the early 1950s.

Nuns at Thornton College and Franciscan monks at St Bernadine's College, Buckingham, have made a fine contribution to education in the district. Sadly the monks have long gone and their London Road buildings are now part of the university. But as we can see from this 1984 picture, the Thornton nuns are still with us. On this occasion, their fête yielded £2,300 profit, much of it thanks to Sister Margaret and the spirit of the bottle store.

Proud parents and guests watch the children dancing at the end of the summer term, 1930s. Leaving this pleasant private school in Chandos Road was quite an ordeal for many – the senior school did not provide as much individual attention.

Young mothers relax at Winslow Hospital. With the war behind them they were able to hope for a peaceful future. The baby on the right is Grace Durham.

The Band Plays On

Buckingham celebrates its history, in the Old Cattle Market, summer 1994. (©
Buckingham and Winslow Advertiser)

Winners of the peace and the nation's future parade down Winslow High Street, late
1940s.

Baroness Thatcher receives an export award from the Lord Lieutenant of Bucks, John Fremantle, at Buckingham University, 1994. Sir Richard Luce, University Vice-Chancellor, looks on. Lady Thatcher accepted the role of chancellor with 'alacrity and enthusiasm' in 1992. (© *Buckingham and Winslow Advertiser*)

Buckingham station lies derelict, late 1960s. Like so many old buildings it has now gone, but memories live on through the words and pictures of the past.

Acknowledgements

Grateful thanks to all who lent me photographs and without whose help there would be no book. Thanks also to those who gave me the words to use; some are mentioned in the text while others have influenced me over the years.

Without Des Tunks I never would have known that the river once ran down Mitre Street or realized the charm of the railways. While larger-than-life characters like Henry Thomas and Bob Tyzack helped me appreciate the more remote corners of the district, Norman Newman illuminated the lost charm of the south.

Without Lorna Joy I would never have met Frank Taylor and his wife, so hospitable, helpful and vivid in their recollections. I could go on but the page would soon run out. So final thanks to the County Library for their usual kindness and permission to reprint pictures, and to the *Buckingham Advertiser* for the same – as well as their hospitality at their offices and so much time spent in their archive.

Here is a list of all who provided photographs; every effort was made to trace copyright owners:

R. Akins • S. Baughan • D. Berry • *Buckingham Advertiser* • Donald Carter
County Library • S. Bennett • R. Dickins • G. Durham • T. Foley
R. Gibbard • G. Harris • D. & E. Lambourne • R. Langley • E. Lowe
N. Newman • B. Owen • C. Phillips • M. Rogers • B. Read • J. Small
Silverstone Racetrack • F. Taylor • H. & E. Thomas • W. Tomkins
D. Tunks • R. Tyzack • V. Wise.

And I nearly forgot: thanks to my own family for pictures and for putting up with me during the preparation of this book.